UP IN THE AIR

The Story of
Bessie Coleman

by Philip S. Hart

Carolrhoda Books, Inc./Minneapolis

WALTHAM FOREST
PUBLIC LIBRARIES

023 399 889

OW | 3 | 11 | 00
6·95

E

920 COL

For my wife, Tanya, and my daughter, Ayanna,
who is now an author in her own right.

This book is available in two editions:
Library binding by Carolrhoda Books, Inc.
Soft cover by First Avenue Editions c/o The Lerner Group
241 First Avenue North, Minneapolis, MN 55401

Text copyright © 1996 by Philip S. Hart
All rights reserved. International copyright secured. No part of this book
may be reproduced, stored in a retrieval system, or transmitted in any form or
by any means, electronic, mechanical, photocopying, recording, or otherwise,
without the prior written permission of Carolrhoda Books, Inc., except for
the inclusion of brief quotations in an acknowledged review.

Library of Congress Cataloging-in-Publication Data
Hart, Philip S.
   Up in the air : the story of Bessie Coleman / by Philip S. Hart.
      p.   cm.
   Includes bibliographical references and index.
   Summary: Presents the story of Bessie Coleman, an American, who in
1920 traveled to France to become the first black woman to earn a pilot's
license.
   ISBN 0–87614–949–2 (library binding) 0–87614–978–6 (paperback)
   1. Coleman, Bessie, 1896–1926—Juvenile literature. 2. Afro-American
air pilots—United States—Biography—Juvenile literature. 3. Women air
pilots—United States—Biography—Juvenile literature. 4. n-us. [1.
Coleman, Bessie, 1896–1926. 2. Air pilots. 3. Afro-Americans—
Biography. 4. Women—Biography.] I. Title.
TL540.C646H37 1996
629.13'092—dc20
[B]   95–32906
                                                                CIP
                                                                 AC

Manufactured in the United States of America
1 2 3 4 5 6 – JR – 01 00 99 98 97 96

Contents

Introduction. 7

1. Dreaming of Flying. 11

2. On to Europe. 31

3. The Barnstorming Life 47

4. Flying High in Florida. 61

   Afterword: The Inspiration. 71

   Notes. 76

   Bibliography 78

   Index 79

   Acknowledgments. 80

Bessie Coleman, the first African-American woman to earn a pilot's
license, shown sometime in the 1920s

Introduction

As I think back over the years that brought me to the point of writing a book for young readers on Bessie Coleman, mixed emotions overcome me. In the 1950s, when I was ten or eleven years of age, my mother, aunt, and grandmother used to show me photographs of James Herman Banning. (Banning was my grandmother's youngest brother.) The three of them would tell me and my brothers and cousins of Banning the pilot. As they told their stories, I used to wonder what and who inspired this young African-American man to fly an airplane back in the mid-1920s.

I can remember going to my school library and to the Denver Public Library trying to find out more about Banning. I found nothing. I began to think my mother, aunt, and grandmother were stretching the truth.

As I grew older, I continued to look for information about Banning, his peers, and those who inspired him. My search proved difficult. My frustration continued throughout my high school years and on into college.

Then in the early 1980s, the Smithsonian Institution's National Air and Space Museum announced that it would be mounting an exhibition on the history of blacks in aviation. With this announcement, all kinds of people like me came forward with photographs and other historical material.

The exhibition *Black Wings* opened in September 1982 at the National Air and Space Museum in Washington, D.C. I was there representing the Banning family along with my younger brother, Christopher Hart, who happens to be a pilot. This was a happy occasion.

With this exhibition, I felt a breakthrough had been achieved. There, I had the opportunity to meet some of Banning's peers. I had the opportunity as well to understand the impact of Bessie Coleman on Banning's desire to become a pilot.

Bessie Coleman was the inspiration for Banning and for hundreds of other black pilots who followed her. In 1921 Coleman was the first black woman to become a licensed pilot.

The great achievements of early black aviators such as Bessie Coleman and James Herman Banning have too long been ignored. For many years, this history had to be held together by individuals like those in my family.

My mother, aunt, and grandmother *were* telling the truth. So was Coleman's nephew, whom I interviewed in his Los Angeles home in 1983. And so were individuals like Marie Dickerson Coker, a black female pilot who followed in Bessie's footsteps, whom I also interviewed.

I used those interviews and my years of research to begin to tell the story of black aviators. Along with my wife,

Tanya, I produced a documentary film on Coleman, Banning, and their peers entitled *Flyers in Search of a Dream.* This film was broadcast on television in 1987.

Since then, there have been more films, historical accounts, and book reprints about Bessie Coleman and other early black aviators. With this book, *Up in the Air: The Story of Bessie Coleman,* I hope to show the truth behind the stories people have held together for so long. And I hope to save young readers the frustration I felt. Today, a ten- or eleven-year-old youngster can go to the library and find books, films, and other materials on Bessie Coleman, James Herman Banning, and other black flyers. This is as it should be.

The earliest known photograph of Bessie Coleman shows her in her twenties.

1

Dreaming of Flying

Bessie Coleman paused on the front porch to watch her younger sisters playing in the yard. She loved Elois, Nilus, and Georgia with all her heart, but looking after them sure was a lot of work. When she wasn't cooking their lunches on the woodstove, Bessie was making sure they'd washed behind their ears, or taking them out back to wade in Mustang Creek.

Nine-year-old Bessie really didn't mind all the work, but she could remember when things had been different. She used to play in the front yard too, by her mother's rosebushes. And she used to go to school every day.

Ever since her father had left and her mother had gone out to work, Bessie had been in charge. She was the one who kept things neat and clean at their house in Waxahachie.

The house Bessie's parents bought near Mustang Creek was like other homes in the black section of Waxahachie, Texas—small, simple, and neat.

Bessie Coleman was born into a large family in Atlanta, Texas, on January 26, 1892. The family moved to the mostly black section of Waxahachie, Texas, just two years later. Bessie's mother, Susan, was African American. Her father, George, was mixed—part African American and part Choctaw or Cherokee.

When Bessie was growing up, American society was strictly segregated. Black children and white children did not go to school together, did not live in the same neighborhoods, and did not have the same opportunities. It was a hard life for black families. Bessie's family was no different from others in this regard. If anything, Mr. Coleman's mixed heritage made it even harder for him to find work.

Because of these difficulties, Bessie's father left his family in Texas in 1901. Frustrated by his situation,

George Coleman went back to Oklahoma, or Indian Territory as it was called then, to find better opportunities. Unable to convince his wife and children to go with him, George Coleman left with a heavy heart.

Susan Coleman found work as a domestic, or maid, in white households around Waxahachie to support the family. Bessie, at age nine, was the oldest child still at home, so she looked after her three younger sisters while her mother worked. Other older Coleman children, including two of Bessie's older brothers who lived up north in Chicago, had already moved on.

Watching Elois, Nilus, and little Georgia wasn't all hard work. Sometimes it was even fun. But it never quite made up for missing school. Bessie had always been an interested and hardworking student. She was eager to learn new things. In the small, crowded classroom at Waxahachie's all-black school, Bessie Coleman stood out as the pretty, petite youngster who did well in nearly all subjects. She was particularly good at math and could do sums in her head faster than most of the other students.

Until her youngest sisters could make the four-mile walk to school with her, Bessie would be going there only occasionally. Between watching her younger sisters and picking cotton during harvesttime, however, Bessie didn't have much time to think about all she was missing.

Late each summer, when the white tufts of cotton stood ready for picking, black families all around Waxahachie gathered to work in the fields. So many children helped out that the black school often closed until after the harvest was done.

Throughout the south, when cotton was ready for picking, entire families went into the fields. Bessie dreaded the hot, backbreaking work.

Working in the cotton fields convinced Bessie of one thing—she did not want to spend the rest of her life picking cotton. It was hot and humid in the fields. The sun bore down on the workers, and the days were very long. The cotton sacks were heavy, especially for one as petite as Bessie.

Even though Bessie didn't much like working in the fields, she knew the family needed her there. She had a hard time dragging the heavy sacks, but she had one skill that came in very handy. Bessie knew sums and math so well that none of the landowners around Waxahachie would dare underpay the Colemans.

One way to be sure of staying out of the cotton fields was to get more education. When her sisters were older, Bessie went back to school. All that time away hadn't dampened her enthusiasm for learning. Bessie did well enough in high school to attend college. Attending college was pretty unusual then, particularly for a black person. But, as people who knew her often said, Bessie's personality seemed to propel her toward the unusual.

In 1910 she enrolled in the all-black Langston Industrial College in Langston, Oklahoma. Langston College was founded upon the principle that hard work on the part of the Negro would lead to progress in America. These were the same guiding principles Booker T. Washington had preached when he had formed the all-black Tuskegee Institute in Alabama.

Surely Bessie was a hard worker. She had completed high school with better than average grades despite caring for her younger sisters and picking cotton. Bessie did not know exactly what she wanted to do when she left home for more schooling. But she knew it had to be better than the life she had been used to.

Knowing her life would be better once she had a college education didn't stop Bessie from being homesick. Langston was miles from home. Sleeping in a bed other than her own back in Waxahachie, Texas, meant Bessie barely slept at all. She missed her mother and sisters.

When she enrolled in Langston Industrial College in 1910, Bessie wasn't ready to take college-level classes. Instead, she studied at the college's preparatory school, gaining skills she'd missed out on at Waxahachie's small all-black school.

At times, Bessie wondered if going to college was the right thing to do after all. When her worries kept her from sleeping, Bessie stayed up late doing schoolwork. For her writing course, Bessie's instructor had the students read newspaper articles and rewrite them in their own words. One article Bessie was rewriting was about the Wright brothers—Orville and Wilbur—famous aviators who had taken the first powered flight at Kitty Hawk, North Carolina, in 1903.

In 1910 flying was still a new and exciting adventure. Bessie and other students in her writing class were wide-eyed when they read about adventurers like the daring Wright brothers or Raymonde de Laroche, a French-woman who had recently become the first licensed female pilot. Bessie had been surprised to learn that women flew, but the reaction of some of her friends and class-mates surprised her even more.

Many people in the early 1900s thought that women had no business sitting behind the controls of an airplane. Flying was dangerous, they said, and women belonged at home. But such talk didn't impress Bessie much. She knew that women were capable of all kinds of things. At least *she* meant to do something unusual with her life.

Whenever Bessie had a minute to spare, she often found herself thinking about flying like a bird. What a wonderful feeling that must be, Bessie thought.

Later that same school year, Bessie came across another surprise. In her mathematics class, Bessie learned from the instructor that an American woman had earned a pilot's license. Her name was Harriet Quimby. Bessie longed to find out more about Quimby and her flights, but studying was more important.

Bessie's classes were going well during her first term at Langston. She wrote to her mother and sisters back in Waxahachie on a regular basis. They were proud of Bessie, but it was evident things at home were not going smoothly with Bessie gone. As the year went on, Susan Coleman was able to send less and less money to her daughter. Bessie was barely able to afford her books.

Would she be able to remain in school much longer? And how could she concentrate on her schoolwork, thinking about her mother's and sisters' needs? Bessie's grades suffered because of the financial pressure. The cotton harvest at home had been bad, so there was no money to send for Bessie's tuition. Soon she was forced to quit school. With her spirits down, Bessie headed back home less than a year after she had begun her studies.

Before leaving school, Bessie probably wrote to her older brother Walter in Chicago. Walter had been living in Chicago for several years with his wife, Willie. Bessie must have told Walter of having to quit school and of not wanting to go back home. If she couldn't go to college, could she come to Chicago instead?

Still waiting to hear from Walter, Bessie arrived back in Waxahachie with mixed feelings. When Bessie told her mother she wanted to go to Chicago, Susan Coleman wasn't too sure of the plan. Bessie, she insisted, was needed at home.

Looking at how hard her mother worked to keep the family together, Bessie couldn't argue. Reluctantly, she settled back into life in Waxahachie. Working as a maid for white families, Bessie earned and saved money. During this time, she also figured how much a one-way ticket to Chicago would cost—but she didn't tell her mother. She *did* tell her sister Georgia and swore her to secrecy.

After long days doing laundry and cooking, Bessie would arrive home and flop down on her bed totally worn out. She missed college and longed to do something more with her life than washing and cooking and cleaning. One day she found a surprise. Sitting on her pillow was a letter from her brother Walter in Chicago.

Bessie was so excited she tore the envelope apart to get at the letter. Walter encouraged Bessie. He could give her a place to stay for a while, he wrote. He also thought he could help her find work. Bessie ran to tell Georgia, but she was afraid to tell her mother. She decided to keep her secret until the time was right.

Harriet Quimby, the first American woman to be licensed as a pilot, made headlines not just because of her daring flights but also because of her plum-colored satin flight suit. In 1912, most people thought a woman shouldn't be wearing trousers—or flying an airplane.

That time wasn't too long in coming. While dusting around the house of the family she worked for, Bessie noticed a front-page newspaper article. With a Boston by-line, the article told of Harriet Quimby's death in a plane crash into Dorchester Bay.

Surprised and shocked, Bessie sat down heavily in a dining room chair. She had not really thought of Harriet Quimby for several months. It was 1912. Bessie had just turned twenty. In an unexplained way, Harriet Quimby's death shook Bessie into action.

With Walter's letter in hand, Bessie approached her mother. Trying to speak with a stern, sure voice, Bessie told her mother that she wanted to head north.

Susan Coleman looked at her strong-willed daughter. Mrs. Coleman was well into her fifties and her dreams had passed. With a heavy heart, she nodded her approval. One more child would be leaving home, heading north. She knew she couldn't hold Bessie back any longer.

Even though she wanted to leave for Chicago as soon as possible, Bessie was smart enough to realize she needed to save more money. It took her another three years to save enough money for the trip north. She also wanted to leave some money with her mother and sisters.

Those three years seemed like an eternity to Bessie. When she finally did board the Rock Island Line headed to Chicago, it was anticlimactic. Sitting on a hard bench in the all-black section of the train, Bessie was both scared and excited. She was excited because this was her first train ride. She was scared and angry because the cramped, all-black section of the train was not nearly as comfortable as the rest of the train, reserved for white passengers.

The twenty-four-hour ride to Chicago took forever, Bessie was so anxious to get there. After arriving at the South Side station, Bessie managed to make it to Walter's apartment on Forest Avenue. She was welcomed with open arms by Walter, his wife, Willie, and by another brother, John, and his wife, Elizabeth.

Walter told Bessie he thought he could get her a job as a maid with a white family on the north side of town. Bessie was grateful for Walter's help, but balked at this suggestion. She hadn't come all the way to Chicago to work for white people just as she had done in Waxahachie.

During the teens and twenties, tens of thousands of southern blacks migrated north in search of greater opportunity. In Chicago, members of this "Great Migration" lived in neighborhoods like this one on the city's South Side.

Walter then told her to check with local barbershops. Bessie was young and attractive, and Walter thought there might be a place for his sister in the grooming business.

Following Walter's suggestion, Bessie learned how to manicure nails. She soon landed a job as a manicurist at the White Sox Barber Shop on Chicago's South Side. Bessie became quite popular in her new profession. She was a favorite manicurist of many young—and not so young—black men in the shop.

In Chicago, she was meeting all kinds of people who wanted to look sharp. Some—bankers, postal workers, and railroad porters like her brother Walter—were in legitimate business. Others, like the local gamblers and thieves, were not.

In the early 1900s, the South Side of Chicago was the center of the black community. Bessie worked and spent most of her free time in an area called the Stroll, which stretched along State Street for nine blocks from Thirty-first to Thirty-ninth Streets. The Stroll had everything a young black woman like Bessie could want—shopping, entertainment, and local gossip. But Bessie came to learn that there was a bigger world beyond Chicago's South Side, and that it was closed off to her because of her race.

Still, to Bessie, Chicago was an exciting place—much more exciting than the small-town life she had left behind. Better yet, she was able to save money and send a bit back home to Waxahachie each month. Her letters to Georgia and the others were full of encouraging words and enthusiasm.

On the Stroll, an area along State Street, South-Side Chicagoans could find everything—from billiard halls to barbershops to nightclubs, such as the Pekin Café pictured above.

Pilot Ruth Law took Chicago by storm in 1916, when she made a record-breaking nonstop flight from that city to Hornell, New York.

In addition to earning her own way, Bessie was meeting eligible young men in the shop and through Walter. She dated a few of them but kept her distance. Bessie began to suspect that Walter wanted her to marry so she would find her own apartment. She knew she wasn't ready to take that step quite yet. Bessie had her dreams, and she didn't think marriage would help her achieve them.

Much as Walter loved his younger sister, he couldn't understand Bessie. He had introduced her to the cream of the South Side crop. Yet she resisted. Any young woman in her right mind would jump at the chance to marry one of these young men, reasoned Walter. But Bessie, he knew, had a mind of her own.

Even with her active life at the shop, meeting young men, and spending time with her family, Bessie occasionally found herself reading and daydreaming. The Chicago papers carried many stories on one of Bessie's favorite topics, flying. Two young white women, Ruth Law and Katherine Stinson, were making headlines flying in Chicago. Sometimes Bessie thought she caught the sound of an airplane engine buzzing overhead. What kind of freedom did people experience when in flight? she wondered. Bessie didn't know what to make of such thoughts, or what they might mean. But she liked the feeling they gave her—a feeling quite different from the busy hum of work and everyday life.

Everyday life had its exciting moments too, however. By 1918 Bessie's mother, Susan, and her sisters, Georgia, Elois, and Nilus, had all moved to Chicago. Bessie had been urging them to move north for some time. She was glad they had finally joined her.

At about the same time, Bessie married an older gentlemen, Claude Glenn, but they never seem to have lived under the same roof. Her family spent time trying to figure out this relationship, but they knew Bessie's independent streak explained it all.

While Bessie adjusted to changes in her life in Chicago, many of her male friends on the South Side were being sent overseas. World War I had been raging in Europe since 1914, the year before Bessie moved north. The United States was drawn into the war in 1917.

At that time, black and white soldiers served in separate units in the U.S. military. Black soldiers were barred from many military jobs—including that of pilot. Because of this racial discrimination, a young African American named Eugene Bullard chose to serve with the French air service during World War I. Bullard could not find a teacher in the United States. He went to France because he had heard that the French were not as racist as white Americans.

Following the custom of the day, pilot Eugene Bullard flew with a small animal on board for luck. His companion on many wartime flights was a pet monkey.

Bullard's exploits flying for the French were well documented in a leading black weekly newspaper, the *Chicago Defender.* Always an avid reader, Bessie was numb with excitement when she first learned about Bullard in the *Defender* in 1918. She had never heard of any black person flying a plane. Bessie would comb through the *Defender* each week to see if there was another story on Bullard's daring flights.

Eugene Bullard would go on to be awarded the *Croix de Guerre,* or Cross of War, the highest honor given by the French military, for his achievements in aviation combat. Bullard inspired Bessie to dream again of flying.

When Bessie went to the movies, she was more eager to see the newsreel footage than the feature itself. She would scan the newsreel for Bullard's face among the many white pilots. Like everything else in American society at that time, movie theaters were segregated. Bessie went to movies at all-black theaters, often watching films produced by all-black companies. The vision of the brave young black pilot, Eugene Bullard, stayed with her.

All during the war, Bessie followed Bullard's story on film, on radio, or in the pages of the *Defender.* One day in the shop, she found herself manicuring the fingernails of the *Defender* editor and publisher, Robert S. Abbott. Abbott, a man in his mid-forties, had founded the *Defender* in 1905. He was an educated, well-dressed, and influential member of Chicago's African-American community. Bessie was hypnotized by the stories Abbott told about Chicago and about prominent members of the South Side community.

Later, when Abbott was again in the shop waiting for his appointment with Bessie, her brother John, who had served in the war, walked in. All the customers and Bessie turned to listen when John began talking about Frenchwomen he had seen and met during wartime. According to John, Frenchwomen talked differently, dressed differently, and walked differently. Some, he claimed, even flew airplanes.

Bessie knew John was only trying to entertain the folks at the barbershop, but his words hit her like a brick. Even though she suspected her brother was stretching the truth, she meant to give flying a try for herself if she could.

In the pages of the widely read *Defender,* editor Robert S. Abbott covered the achievements of African Americans—in Chicago, all across the country, and abroad.

Listening to John talk about Frenchwomen and their planes, Bessie made a decision. She *had* to find someone to teach her to fly like a bird.

Perhaps if Bessie had known how difficult her search would be, she wouldn't have started. The only black pilot she knew about was Eugene Bullard, and he was way over in France. During the next few months, Bessie approached a number of pilots in and around Chicago, all of them white. But all of them gave the same answer. "You're a Negro!" "You're a woman—women have their place, and it's not in the sky!"

Their words rang over and over in Bessie's ears, but she wasn't discouraged. She thought she had a customer who just might be interested in helping her out.

When Bessie Coleman visited Robert Abbott at the *Defender* offices, the busy publisher was willing to make time to hear her story. She had come to seek his advice. How would a woman like herself go about learning to fly? she asked.

Abbott must have been impressed by Coleman's seriousness. He heard her out and then gave her idea some thought. Abbott knew the novelty of a Negro woman pilot could boost readership of the *Defender*. He also knew it would be difficult to find a teacher, due to the rigid separation of the races. Abbott remembered stories of the discrimination Eugene Bullard had faced. Bessie Coleman would face even greater obstacles because of being a woman. In the early 1900s, most people—black or white, male or female—did not believe a woman could, or should, fly a plane.

Abbott told Coleman he needed more time to think about what she had proposed. Then he set an appointment to meet with her at the shop. They would discuss his research while she did his nails.

Bessie was a nervous wreck during the next few days. Time had never moved so slowly. Finally, Robert Abbott strolled in for his weekly manicure. Sitting face-to-face, Coleman buffed Abbott's nails and glanced quickly at his eyes.

Abbott paused, then said in a firm tone that Bessie should go to France. His research confirmed that it would be nearly impossible to find a teacher for her either in the United States or in Canada. The French were much more accepting of both women and Negroes. Plus, the French loved flying. It wasn't going to be easy, but the first step would be learning French. How soon could she start taking lessons?

Bessie would start learning French that very day, if she could just settle down a little. Her emotions were running wild. She almost felt as if she could take off right there—and fly like a bird.

Bessie had this portrait taken while in France.

2

On to Europe

For the next few months Bessie seemed to eat, sleep, and dream French. *"Comment allez-vous aujourd'hui?"* she'd ask Robert Abbott when he walked into the shop for a manicure. Robert chuckled and said he'd been better, but he was truly pleased with her effort.

Weeks passed, and Bessie became more and more comfortable with her French lessons. She also read about French culture. As her language skills improved and her confidence increased, Bessie decided to set a firm deadline for her trip. For some time, she had been saving money. Now, she found out the price for a train ticket to New York and a steamship ticket to Europe.

By this time, she had told Walter, her mother, and her sisters of her plans. Bessie had moved from Walter's apartment to her own small place on Indiana Avenue on the South Side, but she saw her family often. All of them were excited by Bessie's news, but they also worried.

In the 1920s, flying was dangerous. Pilots navigated mostly by guesswork. Airplanes had open cockpits and few instruments. Crashes were common. Pilots were popularly known as "flying fools."

Bessie's family knew the dangers. They saw the difficulty and pain she faced trying to find a teacher. And they worried about Bessie leaving the country. France was so far away!

Even though she loved and respected her family, Bessie refused to allow them to discourage her. She had Robert Abbott's support. She was motivated to amount to something. She had also discussed her plans with Claude Glenn, who went along with her wishes. She *would* go to France and learn to fly.

When she needed advice, Bessie didn't turn to her family. She had come to regard Robert Abbott as her key advisor. In fact, when Robert suggested she take a better-paying job managing a chili parlor, she did just that.

Georgia took over Bessie's manicurist job at the barbershop. Bessie trained her sister herself. While she still did manicures for special customers, Bessie now spent most of her free time working on her French.

By the fall of 1920, Bessie knew where she would be learning to fly; Robert had located a school in France willing to teach her. On November 4, 1920, she applied for her American passport in Chicago. On her application, Bessie gave her age as younger than it actually was. She figured being a black woman pilot would be big news, but being a young black woman pilot might create even bigger waves.

When Bessie Coleman went in to apply for her passport, the clerk put down this description: "twenty-four; five feet, three and half inches in height; a high forehead; brown skin; brown eyes; a sharp nose and medium mouth; a round chin and brown hair."

After leaving her family, friends, and Robert Abbott, Bessie took the train to New York City. On November 20, she boarded the SS *Imparator* and sailed for France. It took a while for Bessie to get used to the voyage. But she did find the other passengers—who were mostly white Americans—to be surprisingly friendly to her. She found this strange, as if leaving the shores of the United States changed their attitudes.

On arriving in France, Bessie first went to Paris looking for the school Abbott had recommended. Finding the school was easy enough, but enrolling as a student was another matter. Two women students had recently died in crashes. Women, the school's instructors concluded, weren't meant to fly. Alone and in a foreign country, Bessie was forced to look for another school. Her task wasn't made any easier by her limited command of French. Despite this limitation, Bessie ended up enrolling at one of France's best aviation schools.

In December of 1920, Bessie Coleman began taking flying lessons at the École d'Aviation des Frères Caudron. Founded by two brothers, pilots and plane builders René and Gaston Caudron, the school was located at Le Crotoy, a small town near the English Channel.

Bessie's lessons included everything from banked turns to looping the loop to aircraft maintenance. She flew a French Nieuport Type 82 biplane. This type of airplane, with two sets of wings stacked one on top of the other, had become popular during World War I. Bessie remembered seeing newsreels of the Nieuport in battle and was excited to be flying the same plane in French skies.

Students at the aviation school run by René and Gaston Caudron posed during a break from flying.

There were days where Bessie had to pinch herself. It was hard to believe she'd left the chili parlor to fly like a bird. That excitement helped her overcome feelings of loneliness. She missed her friends and family, and being the only African American in Le Crotoy made her feel even more alone.

Still, Bessie worked hard. By June she had finished her training and was ready to apply for a pilot's license. That license, issued by the Fédération Aéronautique Internationale, was dated June 15, 1921. The small piece of paper, written in French and showing Bessie's serious face, represented a great achievement. Bessie sent a letter filled with excitement to Robert Abbott. She had reason to be proud. At twenty-nine Bessie Coleman had become the first black woman to earn a pilot's license.

No single piece of paper made Bessie Coleman prouder than her pilot's license, issued by the Fédération Aéronautique Internationale, or International Aeronautical Federation, in 1921.

Her vision and determination had paid off, but Bessie knew she had much to learn. When her courses were over, Bessie left Le Crotoy and headed back to Paris. She hoped to take more lessons at Le Bourget Field just outside the city. Arriving in June, Bessie found the city teeming with tourists from all over Europe and America.

Over the next few months, Bessie continued her flying lessons. She also spent time learning about Paris. She enjoyed everything about the beautiful City of Light. There was something wonderful about being able to move about a city so freely. In Paris, Bessie did not feel hemmed in by invisible racial walls as she had in Chicago. Instead, she felt surrounded by people who loved pilots and planes and flying. Everyone seemed to be interested in aviation.

Bessie knew she would have to return home before long, but in the meantime she continued her lessons at Le Bourget Field. When her money ran low, she made plans for her return trip.

On September 16, 1921, Bessie pushed off from Cherbourg, France, on the SS *Manchuria.* She was on her way home. Only ten short months had passed, but she was a different woman, more mature and worldly than before. With her pilot's license in hand, Bessie set her sights on her next goal, New York City.

When the SS *Manchuria* docked in New York Harbor, Bessie was surprised at the crowd of reporters—both black and white—there to greet her. They came from the *New York Tribune, Aerial Age Weekly, Air Service News,* and others, all to interview Bessie Coleman, the pilot.

As soon as Bessie left the ship, she was surrounded. Other passengers passing the circle of reporters wondered about the confident young black woman at the center. If they didn't already know her story, they would soon.

Robert Abbott had been right. An African-American woman pilot *was* big news. Front-page stories on the young flyer appeared in the *Chicago Defender* and in black-owned newspapers across the country. White-owned newspapers reported on Coleman's accomplishments as well.

Bessie was soon in demand all over New York City. She was guest speaker at several black churches and social clubs. Bessie was also guest of honor at a performance of the musical *Shuffle Along.* The all-black musical had been the rage in New York City that summer.

Bessie's mother posed with the silver cup given to her daughter by the cast of *Shuffle Along* in New York.

Among the *Shuffle Along* cast were Eubie Blake, Noble Sissle, Ethel Waters, and other famous performers.

At intermission Bessie was asked to appear onstage. Ethel Waters presented her with a silver cup engraved with the names of the cast members. The audience was segregated, with white patrons in the better seats and black patrons in the balcony. But both groups applauded Bessie, the first black woman to earn a pilot's license.

As Bessie rode the train back to Chicago from New York, she thought about how far she'd come. She was grateful for the help Robert Abbott had provided her. She wanted to help others—especially young black men and women—the way Abbott had helped her. Sometime early in her flying career, perhaps even as her train glided through Pennsylvania and Ohio, Bessie thought of a way.

She would open her own flight school. She would give flying lessons to anyone who wanted to learn. To Bessie this was a wonderful dream.

When the train pulled into Chicago's Union Station, Bessie glanced out the window. She caught a glimpse of Robert Abbott, as well as her sister Georgia. Bessie pulled her license from her handbag to show them both.

Robert Abbott wanted to be sure that everyone heard the news about Bessie Coleman. First he published a photograph of the license, with its portrait of Bessie in flying gear, in the *Defender.* The following week, the newspaper featured an interview with Bessie. In the interview, she spoke of her desire to open a flight school for black men and women.

Back home on the South Side, she couldn't stop talking about her dreams for the future. Bessie's family was thrilled with her accomplishment, but they worried about the dangers of her new career. In order to raise money for a school, she declared that she was going to stage a series of exhibitions. And exhibition flying, as Bessie's family knew, could be very risky.

By the 1920s, airplanes were no longer novelties. If Bessie wanted to draw crowds, she would have to perform thrilling—and dangerous—stunts. Such stunts were so difficult that Bessie soon decided she needed more training. So, in February 1922, she returned to Europe.

Bessie trained in France for two months and in Germany for ten weeks. She learned to fly more advanced Fokker airplanes and gained a better sense of how to control an airplane in flight. While in Germany, she mingled with the aviation crowd, as well as the elite of German society. She was also filmed flying over the city of Berlin and managed to obtain a copy of the footage.

During her second visit to Europe, Bessie continued her training and met other pilots and airplane manufacturers.

By the first week in August, Bessie was sailing home. When the SS *Noordam* docked in New York on August 13, reporters were there to meet her, just as they had been when she returned from France.

With the financial support of the *Defender,* Bessie was to be the featured attraction on September 3 at an air show on Long Island. Bessie was nervous, but she wanted everyone to hear about her first American flight. She talked to reporters about her plans and stretched the truth a bit to build up excitement. Instead of talking about chili parlors and barbershops, she told one reporter she'd learned to fly in France after going there as a Red Cross nurse.

By the time the Long Island air show came around, she had made waves throughout New York City. Although

Bessie shared the bill that day with parachutist Hubert Fauntleroy Julian, nicknamed "the Black Eagle," most people came to see the first U.S. flight of the country's only licensed black woman pilot.

While testing her borrowed airplane, Bessie wore a simple coverall. When flyers appeared at air shows, however, they were expected to dress up.

A member of the Fifteenth New York Infantry, an all-black unit from World War I, presented flowers to Bessie Coleman on the occasion of her first U.S. flight. The identity of the young boy is unknown.

The Long Island exhibition was such a success that Bessie was soon booked to perform at the Negro Tri-State Fair in Memphis, Tennessee. With another successful exhibition flight behind her and her confidence up, Bessie Coleman was ready to return to Chicago. It was time to show the hometown folks what she could do. She did have one problem to overcome, however. She did not own a plane. Although she had often boasted to reporters about the airplanes she'd ordered in Europe, Bessie still didn't have the money to buy a plane of her own.

Soon after Bessie's return to Chicago, a small item appeared in the *Defender*. It announced an aerial exhibition to be held at Checkerboard Field on October 15, 1922, featuring Chicago's own, Bessie Coleman. Murmurs of excitement swept through the South Side community. The *Defender* offices were swamped with messages.

Despite her outward calm and bravado, Bessie was very nervous. She was still a novice pilot. And this exhibition would be in front of her family and friends—and a sizable hometown crowd. She didn't want to let them down, but sometimes she wondered if her family was correct. Should she quit now and be satisfied with having earned her license?

As self-doubt threatened to overwhelm her, Bessie approached Robert. He did his best to calm her fears. After considerable soul-searching, Bessie decided to go ahead. She had spent enough time in the air to know she wanted to fly for a living. Even though Bessie could earn money by managing a chili parlor, she didn't choose that route. She loved flying too much to consider any other way.

Before long, Bessie was spending hours at Checkerboard Field, familiarizing herself with a borrowed biplane and prepping it for the exhibition. When October 15, 1922, dawned, it was a glorious fall day. The Chicago airfield was packed with both black and white spectators. Among the buzzing crowd was Bessie's eight-year-old nephew from Flint, Michigan, Arthur Freeman. Arthur was there with his mother, Nilus, along with most of the other family members.

Young Arthur wanted to ride with his aunt Bessie, but so did a long line of other people, relatives and strangers. They were all hoping to fly with the famous pilot, even though the price was steep at five dollars a ride.

Over the course of her first air shows, Bessie experimented with different outfits, many of which looked like military uniforms.

To Arthur and to others in the crowd, Bessie seemed fearless. Sitting in the open cockpit, her scarf flowing behind her in the wind, Bessie waved to the crowd and performed all kinds of stunts.

For a finale, she pulled back on the control stick and aimed the plane skyward as the engine strained. Even when it seemed she couldn't go any higher, Bessie continued to press the biplane up. When the plane reached the limit of its climb, the engine suddenly faltered and died. The crowd fell silent below, convinced this was the end of Bessie Coleman and her borrowed plane. Everyone craned to see the inevitable crash.

As the plane plummeted closer and closer to the ground, people scattered. At the last possible moment, Bessie allowed the air rushing over the propeller to kick the engine back to life. Bessie hauled back the stick for all she was worth and brought the plane out of its dive. When the biplane shot over their heads, people went crazy. After making a victory roll for the folks, Bessie touched down and taxied up to the gathering crowd.

Bessie herself was amazed at the skills she'd shown that fall day. Her self-doubt had eased somewhat, and, on top of that, the air show had earned almost one thousand dollars. Bessie opened up an account at the black-owned Binga State Bank. There she would begin saving for a first payment on her flight school and for her expenses.

Everywhere Bessie went in Chicago's black community she was mobbed for her autograph, or her scarf, or just a smile. Bessie's natural charm and good looks fit perfectly with her newfound role as local heroine. For the time being anyway, she did not have to worry about going back to work at the chili parlor or the barbershop. She was in demand as a paid speaker at black churches and social clubs throughout Chicago.

Because her exploits were covered by other black-owned newspapers like the *Pittsburgh Courier* and the *California Eagle,* Bessie's fame was spreading. Her mail was full of invitations to speak in other parts of the country.

As Bessie plotted her next move with Robert Abbott, Georgia and the rest of her family were being won over to Bessie's side. They were scared, yet proud, of her Checkerboard Field debut. Bessie, they realized, had found something she truly loved. Opportunities to earn money flying in Chicago were limited, however. In order to raise money to open her own school, Bessie would have to barnstorm other parts of the country. It was time, she decided, to spread her wings and to spread the gospel of blacks in aviation.

3

The Barnstorming Life

Bessie had realized while in France that just having a license to fly would not guarantee a job as a pilot. At that time, commercial airlines taking passengers from city to city were still in the future. The U.S. airmail service employed pilots, but only white men. Most pilots, whether they had a license or not, were forced to live by their wits.

In the 1920s, traveling pilots would take brave souls up in the air for a fee. They would try to find work at county fairs adding some aerial thrills. And they would comb the countryside looking for short-hop passengers and for deliveries. Often they would be forced down in fields or in farmlands when fuel ran low or when the sun went down. They might even find themselves sleeping in barns at night. Barnstormers, as people called them, stormed the countryside, looking for ways to earn a living. It was not a safe life, but these "flying fools" were risk takers and adventurers. When Bessie took up the barnstorming life, she was no different.

Barnstormers performed stunts ranging from wing walking to parachute jumping to looping the loop.

After the publicity died down from the Checkerboard Field exhibition, Bessie set her sights on California. Los Angeles, she thought, would be a great place to pursue her dream. The growing western city was becoming the center of the nation's emerging aviation and movie industries. Soon Bessie was discussing plans for a trip west.

Bessie left wintry Chicago in late January 1923. She headed first to Oakland. She was seeking an endorsement deal with the Coast Tire and Rubber Company, located in that Bay Area city. Under the deal, Bessie would represent Coast Tire at public events and put their corporate logo on the planes she flew. Several white pilots had similar endorsement deals, but Bessie was the first black flyer to make such an agreement with a major corporation.

After completing this arrangement with Coast Tire, she headed south for Los Angeles. The African-American population in Los Angeles had increased rapidly between 1910 and 1920. Many were attracted to the city during World War I by jobs in factories that produced airplanes and military equipment. By the time Bessie arrived, the Central Avenue community of Los Angeles had a black YMCA, a black YWCA, a black hospital, and five black newspapers. There were also several social clubs and black churches. Los Angeles attracted many of the best educated and most prominent African Americans in the United States. And now Bessie was among the most prominent.

Bessie Coleman felt welcomed by the black community of Los Angeles. There, many African Americans, like the Central Avenue pharmacist pictured above, owned their own businesses.

Bessie's first airplane, a Curtiss JN-4, or Jenny, was made mainly of wires, wood, and canvas. Jennies were cheap and relatively easy to fly, but even with careful maintenance the gasoline-powered engines often stalled in flight.

Bessie's reputation had preceded her. The *California Eagle,* the best known of the five black newspapers in the area, had covered her adventures over the past year.

Once in Los Angeles, Bessie purchased an airplane, a Curtiss JN-4, for about $400. Most of the purchase price came from her Coast Tire advance payment. Her "new" airplane was an old World War I biplane, commonly called a Jenny. Many Jennies had been produced as training planes during the war. Now the surplus airplanes were quite popular with aviation enthusiasts, mainly because they were cheap.

Many of the flyers in the Los Angeles area flew Jennies. This put Bessie at ease. So did Los Angeles, with its growing businesses scattered along Central Avenue. Going west, Bessie decided, was the right choice. And perhaps Los Angeles was the right place to start her aviation school.

Ever conscious of the press, Bessie made a point of visiting with all the local black newspapers to tell them of her plans. Sometimes prone to exaggeration, Bessie painted a very ambitious picture of an aviation school for blacks, complete with a fleet of top-notch airplanes.

The truth could hardly be more different. Once Bessie's lone plane—the recently purchased Jenny—was ready, she attempted to set up an exhibition flight at Rogers Field in Los Angeles. But when her backers pulled out at the last moment, Bessie's plans fell through. Coast Tire had helped her buy the Jenny, but they refused Bessie more support.

Bessie spent the next few weeks scrambling for new backers. Finally, she succeeded in finding enough support to schedule another exhibition. Set for February 4, 1923, this exhibition would take place at Palomar Park near Slauson Avenue. Bessie was sure she would draw a good crowd since she had gotten good publicity since arriving in Los Angeles.

This time everything seemed to be working out just right. Bessie was to be the sole attraction at Palomar Park. Long before Bessie was due to fly, nearly 10,000 people had gathered at the park. Bessie's excitement was matched by that of the large, and largely black, crowd.

To gain backing for exhibitions, Bessie wrote many letters. Her writing paper showed her portrait and a sample of her more daring stunts.

When Bessie took off from Santa Monica where her plane had been parked, she felt confident. The plane had been newly conditioned and the park was only a short hop away. While the biplane rose above the city streets, Bessie went over her plans for the air show. She would try another dead motor landing just as she had at Checkerboard Field, along with other stunts.

But soon after takeoff, Bessie's planning ended. The Jenny's motor stalled, and the biplane began a quick fall, nose first, to the streets below. Bessie tried to pull out of the dive but failed. The Jenny hit the ground, and its pilot lay motionless.

Bessie was lucky the Jenny was flying at only 300 feet when the motor stalled. When she was pulled out of the wreckage, she was still alive but unconscious. A doctor at the site of the crash did what he could, but Bessie had to be transported to Saint Catherine's Hospital in Santa Monica. After she came to, Bessie discovered that she had broken one leg and fractured several ribs. Her face showed cuts and bruises, and there were internal injuries as well. This was her first crash. She hoped she never had another.

Bessie would have plenty of time to think about the dangers of her chosen career while she was being patched up and cared for at the hospital. She was in pain from her injuries, from losing her only airplane, and, perhaps worst of all, from letting down the thousands of spectators who had awaited her arrival at Palomar Park in Los Angeles.

As Bessie was rushed to the hospital, spectators at Palomar Park had grown angry. Many had demanded a refund of their money. Bessie could hardly blame them. She hated disappointing her fans. Once she was able, she sent a telegram, saying, "TELL THEM ALL THAT AS SOON AS I CAN WALK I'M GOING TO FLY!"

Meanwhile, word of Bessie's crash reached Chicago. Susan Coleman, Elois, Georgia, and the others were all concerned and worried. Bessie soon sent word to her family and friends that she was going to be fine. But she was not free from worry.

Her broken leg was taking far longer to heal than she had planned. As she recuperated in the hospital over the next few weeks, Bessie continued to plot and plan. The crash had been a setback, no doubt about it. But nothing was going to stop her from opening a flying school.

It was May of 1923 when Bessie finally hobbled out of the hospital on crutches. For the balance of that month, she stayed at a friend's home in Los Angeles. She gave a few lectures and showed films of her earlier flights. By June, however, Bessie was ready to head back to Chicago. She was without a plane. Her pockets were empty. Her nearly six-month stay in sunny California had proven to be less than profitable.

Bessie's sisters, Elois and Nilus, were glad to have her back home in Chicago. Bessie's accident, however, troubled the family deeply.

Even being broke did not discourage Bessie for long. Once back in Chicago, she arranged to be part of an air show in Columbus, Ohio, on Labor Day. When day broke and rain poured down, Bessie's heart sank as well. Another show had been canceled. Another crowd had been let down.

Bessie retreated back to Chicago until the following weekend. She hoped her luck might change at the rescheduled air show.

There was an upbeat crowd at the fairground on that September day. Bessie was pretty good at estimating crowds by now; she was sure at least 10,000 people were there. There was also plenty of sunshine. All in all, Bessie couldn't have hoped for a better day. Her borrowed plane responded easily. And her spirits received the lift they so desperately needed.

Back in Chicago after this triumph, Bessie was full of plans. Soon, she told a reporter from the *Chicago Defender,* she was going to give a farewell flight to her hometown. Then, she would barnstorm the south.

But although her fans waited expectantly, nothing happened. No farewell flight nor southern tour came to be, and Bessie's boasting cost her some fans and friends. To make matters worse, her string of bad luck had cooled her first supporter, Robert Abbott. He let her know he was no longer interested in promoting her many plans and adventures. She had disappointed him by setting up expectations she could not meet.

Bessie settled into an apartment on South Parkway to rest and regroup. Despite her achievements, she found that she did not fit into Chicago's black middle-class society. To many black Chicagoans such as Robert Abbott, Bessie Coleman seemed too unpredictable.

Bessie's family, however, was happy to have her home again. Her apartment became the gathering place for sisters, brothers, nieces, and nephews. Bessie was a world traveler, a famous flyer, and a hero. She had done more than any other Coleman had ever done! Her nieces and nephews loved to hear her stories.

This normal life suited Bessie fine for a while. Then in early 1925, she felt she had to move on. Her dreams had not died, despite the setbacks.

Thirty-three years after her birth, Bessie decided to gear up and head back to Texas. In the years since she had left her home state, Bessie had indeed amounted to something. The former cotton picker and maid was now the only licensed African-American woman pilot in the whole world. She was fluent in French. She was a world traveler. She was polished. Yet she was returning to Texas to launch a comeback. Bessie Coleman was trying to escape the bad luck that seemed so eager to follow her. The city of Houston would be her new base of operations.

On May 9, 1925, Bessie gave her first lecture in Houston. Along with a short speech, she showed films of her flights. With this type of presentation, she was able to raise enough money to cover her expenses and save a few dollars for a new plane. Her experiences were unique, and the Houston audience seemed to like her. Over the next few weeks, Bessie gave several lectures. All the audiences were receptive and eager to meet her.

Five weeks after she arrived in Houston, Bessie took her first flight. She had to borrow a plane, but she was determined to get off the ground. The air show was set for June 19, or Juneteenth, in the African-American community. This was the date in 1865 when blacks in Texas had achieved their freedom after the Civil War.

Publicity photographs, like this undated portrait with a Jenny, were likely to be printed in black-owned newspapers in areas where Bessie made her flights.

Again, Bessie's reputation preceded her. The stands were full of white spectators—while the black audience stood on a dirt surface. People of both races were eager to see the famous Bessie Coleman fly an airplane.

Bessie performed magnificently, just as she had done in her Chicago exhibition at Checkerboard Field and later in Columbus. She performed many of her usual stunts, adding barrel rolls and figure eights. Her accident in California some two years earlier did not seem to have made her any less daring.

Thousands of fans had a glorious Juneteenth in Houston that year, thanks to Bessie Coleman. Many of her bravest fans paid for the chance to ride in the plane with Queen Bess herself.

At that time in Texas, it was still unusual to see an airplane, much less an airplane piloted by a black woman. So many people were curious to see her that Bessie hoped to make a fairly good living there.

Over the next few weeks, she made appearances in Houston, San Antonio, Dallas, Fort Worth, and smaller towns in between—including Waxahachie, Bessie's old hometown. At each of these stops, Bessie was either lecturing or flying.

Early in the fall of 1925, Bessie returned home to Chicago for a break. She wanted to see her family and rest up a bit. She had money in the bank. Her mind and body were fully healed. She was healthy, high-spirited, and feeling confident once again.

After a three-month stay, Bessie was ready to go back on the road—a life she had grown to love. She would soon be lecturing again, this time in Georgia and Florida. Bessie spent Christmas Eve 1925 with Elois, wrapping gifts and talking through the night. Then she left for Savannah, Georgia.

Her first lecture was at a local theater. The black weekly *Savannah Tribune* told of the community's excitement at hosting this famous visitor. Bessie gave lectures in Augusta and Atlanta as well. She then headed for Florida, where she spoke and showed films of her flights in Saint Petersburg, Tampa, and West Palm Beach. At this rate, with the profits from her Texas tour and a successful Florida trip, she would soon be close to her goal. She might even have enough money by spring to open her own school.

During her barnstorming tours of the south, Bessie made many friends, one of whom is pictured with her here.

4

Flying High in Florida

Bessie's lectures were proving to be popular. She was drawing crowds at all her stops. But she didn't let success slow her search for new ways to raise money for her school. The films she showed of her earlier flights were so popular that Bessie was seriously thinking about having a movie made about her flights and career.

In 1926 the movie industry, like the aviation industry, was in its infancy. In addition to movies made in Hollywood, black and white filmmakers in cities across the country were also producing race movies. These movies were meant for black audiences. They were often shown at midnight, when whites were not using the theater. Or they were shown in black-owned movie theaters.

Bessie wrote to a producer of race movies in February of 1926. In a letter to Norman Studios in Arlington, Florida, Bessie expressed her desire to put her life on film. She was convinced a movie on her life would be a big hit. After all, her story was unique, full of adventure, and sure to draw her many fans.

In her letter to the owner of Norman Studios, a producer of race films, Bessie boasted, "Yes Mr. Norman I am more than *sure* my picture will go big in colored [movie] houses."

When nothing came of Bessie's movie career with Norman Studios, she didn't get too discouraged. Instead, she continued lecturing. She worked part-time in a beauty parlor in Orlando, Florida, and flew as often as she could to raise money to open her school. But getting up in the air proved a constant struggle.

Bessie did not own a plane while in Florida. In fact, she hadn't owned one since she crashed her Jenny in California. Whenever she flew in Chicago, Florida, or Texas, Bessie had to borrow a plane. This limited her ability to fly in air shows and to take people up for rides. It also limited her ability to earn money. Still, Bessie did manage to give an exhibition using a borrowed airplane in West Palm Beach early in 1926.

Often Bessie was able to borrow a plane from local white pilots. For some reason, white pilots seemed less racist than other whites. Perhaps because they shared a special bond—a love of flying—white and black flyers felt a kinship not found in the rest of society.

Some months before, Bessie had made a down payment on a plane of her own in Dallas. Try as she might, Bessie couldn't find the money to pay it off. So while a Curtiss Jenny sat waiting for her in Dallas, Bessie scrambled to discover some way to raise more funds so she could get her plane to Florida.

In February of 1926, Bessie met Edwin M. Beeman, heir to the Beeman chewing gum fortune. When Beeman gave her money to make the final payment on her plane in Dallas, the young pilot thought her troubles were over. With Beeman's support, Bessie made arrangements to have her plane flown to Jacksonville, Florida. The Jacksonville Negro Welfare League had invited her to perform there on May 1, and she planned to use her new plane.

The Jacksonville train station had separate waiting rooms for black and white passengers.

Jacksonville, like most Florida cities, was completely segregated. Blacks and whites lived and worked separately. All the same, the white newspaper in Jacksonville ran a story announcing Bessie's upcoming exhibition.

Bessie was also making headlines in the black community. She was booked for a number of speaking engagements in churches and theaters, and at local all-black public schools. Increasingly, Bessie was taking her message to black children. They seemed more eager to learn about flying than adults—and more likely to enroll in her school.

While Coleman was on her way to Jacksonville, a young white mechanic named William D. Wills was leaving Love Field in Dallas. Wills had agreed to pilot the

Jenny. Although the plane was new to Coleman, it was even older than the first Jenny she had owned in California. This was the type of airplane she had to settle for. Without more money coming in on a regular basis, Bessie could never afford anything better, newer, or safer.

Even during the short flight from Dallas to Jacksonville, the plane had problems. Wills had to land in Meridian, and Farmingdale, Mississippi. At each stop, he made repairs to the struggling Jenny. Despite these problems, Wills landed in Jacksonville on April 28. Local pilots who met Wills were surprised that he had managed to pilot the old plane so far.

For a fee, William D. Wills agreed to fly Bessie Coleman's new airplane from Dallas, Texas, to Jacksonville, Florida.

On April 30, Coleman met Wills at Paxon Field in Jacksonville to try out the Jenny. She was looking forward to flying her own plane at last. Coleman and Wills planned to fly over a nearby racetrack, the site of the next day's exhibition for the Negro Welfare League.

For one of her planned stunts, Bessie would be trying something different, a parachute jump from the wings of the Jenny. So for their trial run, William Wills took over the controls, while Bessie sat behind him. The Jenny rose high above Jacksonville, climbing to 2,000 and then to 3,500 feet. Wills circled so Coleman could view the racetrack and then turned back.

Suddenly the plane accelerated, and the Jenny began a quick, spinning dive toward the ground. William Wills tried to regain control of the spiraling Jenny, but to no avail. As the plane spun downward, Bessie was thrown from her seat. Like most flyers of her day, she didn't wear a seat belt. She fell to her death. William Wills stayed at the controls until the Jenny crashed onto farmland not far from where Bessie Coleman's crushed body lay. Wills died soon afterward.

Coleman's body was taken to a local black-owned funeral home. Wills's body was taken to a white-owned funeral home.

Meanwhile, officials searched for, and found, the cause of the accident. A wrench had slid into the control gears. The gears had jammed, thus disabling the plane. Local aviators said that the accident would not have happened had Bessie been piloting a newer plane, whose gears would have been covered.

After rushing to the scene of the crash, a nervous and upset organizer for the Negro Welfare League's air show lit a cigarette and accidentally set the wreckage on fire. William Wills died in the flames. Bessie Coleman's body was found 1,000 feet away.

However, Bessie had no choice. She wanted to fly. As with many other things in a segregated society, a black person often has to make do with second best, sometimes with deadly results. Bessie had faced this fact her whole life, but she didn't let it hold her back. To her death, she had resisted society's boundaries for blacks and for women.

Bessie Coleman, 1892–1926

Bessie's body lay in state in Jacksonville. A memorial service was held at which nearly 5,000 people mourned brave Queen Bess. A memorial service was also held in Orlando. Then Bessie's body was sent by train to Chicago to be with her family.

For the service at the Pilgrim Baptist Church in Chicago in May of 1926, nearly 1,500 family, friends, and fans crowded the pews. Outside, thousands more milled about, unable to get in.

Many words were spoken to honor Bessie Coleman, but she is perhaps best remembered in this anonymous verse:

> High up into the azure skies,
>> Amid the April clouds,
> The man-invented plane-bird flies,
>> Above the watching crowds.
> With steady hand the pilot guides,
>> and higher up it goes.
> Upon the milky way it glides,
>> And earth a greeting throws.
> A sudden nosedive in the air,
>> A guiding hand astray,
> And fate has worked its wicked snare,
>> On April's last spring day.
> Through a space a pilot falls to earth,
>> And in the field lies dead.
> Around are stilled the shouts of mirth,
>> While silent tears are shed.

Afterword

The Inspiration

Among the pallbearers, speakers, and mourners at Bessie Coleman's final memorial were the finest of Chicago's African-American community. Bessie had arrived by train from Texas in 1915 as an unknown cotton picker. She was eulogized eleven years later as a shining light the world over. Junius C. Austin, the Pilgrim Baptist Church pastor, said of Bessie Coleman in his remarks, "This girl was one hundred years ahead of the Race she loved so well. . . ."

Bessie Coleman, Eugene Bullard, Harriet Quimby, and other early pilots were on the cutting edge of a new industry. But unlike other pilots, Bessie had to overcome the problem of being both a woman and an African American. Even with these dual handicaps, Bessie Coleman pursued her dream. From humble beginnings in Texas to her death as a celebrated aviator in Florida, she paved the way for others to follow. Bessie Coleman was an inspiration for African-American men and women for years to come.

Coleman's dream of a flying school for African Americans became a reality at the Bessie Coleman Aero Club in Los Angeles, California. William J. Powell founded the school.

Among those inspired by her example was William J. Powell. Powell was with the other mourners crowded outside the Pilgrim Baptist Church at Coleman's funeral. He owned several service stations and a garage in Chicago. A World War I veteran, Powell had taken his first airplane ride not long before, while at a convention in Paris, France. Since that first flight, Powell—like Bessie Coleman years earlier—had been bitten by the aviation bug.

Powell had followed Bessie's career closely. He had read everything he could about her, whether in the *Defender,* the *California Eagle,* the *Pittsburgh Courier,* or other newspapers. Soon after Coleman's burial in 1926, Powell decided to sell his Chicago businesses and move to Los Angeles. He wanted to be where the aviation action was. Once he had learned to fly, Powell carried on Bessie's dream of opening an aviation school for African Americans. Using his skills as a businessman, Powell and others opened the Bessie Coleman Aero Club in Los Angeles in 1929.

James Herman Banning from Ames, Iowa, was the school's chief instructor and the most experienced African-American pilot at that time. He had earned his license in 1926 from the U.S. Department of Commerce, becoming the first African American to do so.

Among Banning's students was Marie Dickerson, a noted dancer and singer. Dickerson was performing at a nightclub in Culver City, California, in the late 1920s. Looking through the *California Eagle* one day, Dickerson came across an advertisement for the Bessie Coleman Aero Club at 1423 West Jefferson Boulevard. She could not believe her eyes. Not only was there a school for blacks—but it was named after a black woman. When she came to Los Angeles, Marie approached the school's storefront office with a sense of pride.

Through her lessons at the Bessie Coleman Aero Club, Marie soon earned her license. She became a member of the Five Blackbirds, a flying troupe that performed at air shows. The Five Blackbirds performed at the very first all-black air show in October 1931 at the Eastside Airport in Los Angeles, and the Bessie Coleman Aero Club sponsored that historic event.

To honor Bessie Coleman's memory, black pilots in the Chicago area began a tradition of flying over Coleman's grave, located just outside the city at Lincoln Cemetery in Blue Island, Illinois.

Perhaps the most important milestone of the Bessie Coleman Aero Club occurred in 1932. Banning and twenty-five-year-old ace mechanic Thomas C. Allen completed the first transcontinental flight by black pilots. Banning and Allen left Los Angeles in a secondhand biplane on September 18 and landed in New York on October 9, 1932. Nicknamed the Flying Hobos, the two landed in New York not as hobos, but as heroes.

Graduates of the Bessie Coleman Aero Club weren't the only pilots to follow the trail Bessie Coleman blazed. An aviation school mainly for African Americans was formed in Chicago in the early 1930s. The Chicago school also recognized Bessie Coleman as its inspiration. Among those affiliated with the school were Cornelius Coffey, John Robinson, Willa Brown, and Harold Hurd. This group first started the tradition of flying over Bessie's grave each Memorial Day and dropping a floral wreath in her honor. That tradition continues.

Nearly seventy years after her death, Bessie Coleman's life is still remembered and honored. And she is still inspiring others to fly, including Dr. Mae Jemison, the first African-American woman astronaut.

In many ways, Bessie Coleman was the Amelia Earhart of the African-American community. Unlike Earhart, Coleman did not have the support that could have made her brief career even more memorable. Thus, while Amelia Earhart flew top-notch airplanes, Bessie Coleman had to be content with secondhand, rebuilt Jennies.

Despite such discrimination, Bessie did not allow herself to become bitter. She kept her dream in mind. She also realized that her mission was to encourage other African Americans to get into aviation on the ground floor.

Bessie Coleman wasn't perfect. She made mistakes. She made enemies. And she never saw her dream come true. However, her impact is still being felt today. Those individuals Bessie Coleman inspired have helped make her dream a reality. To this day, African Americans are trying to gain equal access to resources—whether in aviation, business, or other fields of endeavor. Bessie Coleman's story tells us all that no matter how humble our beginnings, if we dare to dream, we can succeed.

Notes

page 12

Bessie had no birth certificate and frequently lied about her age, so it is difficult to know for certain when she was born. The date January 26, 1892, is found in the only full-length biography of Bessie, *Queen Bess: Daredevil Aviator,* by Doris L. Rich.

page 43

Arthur Freeman was only eight years old when he saw his aunt Bessie Coleman fly at Checkerboard Field. Years later, however, his memories of that day were still fresh. In an interview, Freeman recalled in detail the daring stunts that his aunt performed that October day. He was disappointed that he couldn't ride with Coleman, but the line was too long even at the high asking price. "At that time," Freeman recalled, "I think it was $5 a ride."

In spite of his disappointment, Arthur Freeman later followed his brave aunt into the skies. Freeman became a licensed pilot.

page 51

Rogers Field in Los Angeles was the same airfield where Amelia Earhart had taken her first flight as a passenger in 1921.

page 63

The motives of Edwin M. Beeman, a white man, in supporting Bessie Coleman's career are unclear. The interests of Coleman's first supporter, Robert Abbott, are more evident. Abbott supported Coleman early in her career primarily to boost readership in his newspaper, the *Chicago Defender.*

In 1995, the United States Postal Service issued a stamp honoring Bessie Coleman and highlighting her role in black history.

page 69

This poem about Bessie Coleman is reproduced as it was printed in William J. Powell's 1934 book *Black Wings*.

page 73

James Herman Banning, the chief flight instructor at the Bessie Coleman Aero Club, was also inspired by Bessie Coleman's example. After his history-making flight across the United States, Banning continued to fly and to teach flying. He died in San Diego on February 5, 1933, in a crash. He was not piloting the plane but was being flown to another plane that he was to have used to perform aerial stunts for a waiting crowd.

page 73

In an interview, Marie Dickerson Coker recalled when she was first bitten by the aviation bug. In the late 1920s, when Marie was playing the piano at a Culver City, California, nightclub called the Chicken Coop, two men dressed in flying gear walked in. At first, Marie thought they were actors working at the Metro-Goldwyn movie studio down the street. But when she asked the men, they said they were aviators, not actors. Then they asked her if she'd like to go up in their airplane. "Up in a plane? I thought they were kidding," Marie recalled. When she later saw an advertisement for the Bessie Coleman Aero Club, Marie jumped at the chance to become a pilot.

Bibliography

Books:

*Briggs, Carole S. *At the Controls: Women in Aviation.* Minneapolis: Lerner Publications Company, 1991.

Hardesty, Von and Dominick Pisano. *Black Wings: The American Black in Aviation.* Washington: National Air and Space Museum, Smithsonian Institution Press, 1983.

*Hart, Philip S. *Flying Free: America's First Black Aviators.* Minneapolis: Lerner Publications Company, 1992.

*Haskins, Jim. *Black Eagles: African Americans in Aviation.* New York: Scholastic Inc., 1995.

Lynn, Jack. *The Hallelujah Flight.* New York: St. Martin's Press, 1990.

Powell, William J. *Black Aviator: William J. Powell.* Washington: Smithsonian Institution Press, 1994. (Reprint of *Black Wings,* 1934.)

Rich, Doris L. *Queen Bess: Daredevil Aviator.* Washington: Smithsonian Institution Press, 1993.

Films:

Flyers in Search of a Dream. Produced by Philip Hart in association with WGBH-Boston and UCLA. PBS documentary film. 1987.

Interviews with Author:

Coker, Marie Dickerson. Student at Bessie Coleman Aero Club. Los Angeles, CA. September 1983.

Freeman, Arthur. Nephew of Bessie Coleman. Los Angeles, CA. September 1983.

All quotations in this biography were taken from the above sources.

*A star denotes a book for younger readers.

Index

Abbott, Robert S., 26, 27, 28–29, 31, 32, 35, 39, 43, 46, 55, 76

Air shows, 40–42, 43–45, 51–53, 55, 56–58, 63

Banning, James Herman, 7–8, 9, 73, 74, 77

Barnstormers, 46, 47, 48, 55

Beeman, Edwin M., 63, 76

Berlin, Germany, 39

Bessie Coleman Aero Club, 73–74, 77

Bullard, Eugene, 24–26, 27, 28, 71

California Eagle, 46, 50, 72, 73

Caudron, Gaston and René, 34, 35

Checkerboard Field (Chicago), 42, 43–46

Chicago, 18, 20–24, 26–27, 39, 42–46, 54–56, 58

Chicago Defender, 25, 26, 27, 28, 37, 39, 40, 42–43, 72

Coast Tire and Rubber Company (Oakland, CA), 48–49, 50, 51

Coker, Marie Dickerson. *See* Dickerson, Marie

Coleman, Bessie: appearance, 33, 41, 44; birth, 12, 76; childhood, 11–15; crashes, 52–53, 66; death, 66; education, 13, 15, 31; flight training, 34–37, 39; flights, 40–42, 43–45, 51–53, 55, 56–58, 63; marriage, 24; pilot's license, 35, 36; plans for school, 38, 39, 51, 53, 59, 61, 63, 73

Coleman, Elizabeth (sister-in-law), 20

Coleman, Elois (sister), 11, 13, 24, 53, 58

Coleman, George (father), 12–13

Coleman, Georgia (sister), 11, 13, 18, 22, 24, 32, 39, 46, 53

Coleman, John (brother), 20, 26–27

Coleman, Nilus (sister), 11, 13, 24, 43

Coleman, Susan (mother), 12, 13, 17, 18, 19–20, 24, 53

Coleman, Walter (brother), 18, 19, 20–21, 23

Coleman, Willie (sister-in-law), 20

Curtiss JN-4 ("Jenny"), 50–52, 63, 65–66

Dallas, TX, 58, 63

Dickerson, Marie, 8, 73, 77

Discrimination. *See* Racism; Segregation

Earhart, Amelia, 75, 76

École d'Aviation des Frères Caudron (Aviation School of the Caudron Brothers), 34

Exhibitions, flight. *See* Air shows

Fédération Aéronautique Internationale (International Aeronautical Federation), 35

Flyers in Search of a Dream, 9

France, 24–25, 26–27, 28–29, 32, 39. *See also* Paris, France

Freeman, Arthur (nephew), 8, 43, 76

Freeman, Nilus. *See* Coleman, Nilus

Glenn, Claude (husband), 24, 32

Houston, TX, 56–58

Jacksonville, FL, 63–64, 65–66

Jemison, Dr. Mae, 75
"Jenny." *See* Curtiss JN-4
Julian, Hubert Fauntleroy, 41
Juneteenth, 56–58

Langston, OK, 15–17
Langston Industrial College, 15–17
Le Bourget Field (Paris), 36–37
Le Crotoy, France, 34–35, 36
Long Island, NY, 40–42
Los Angeles, CA, 48–51, 54, 73

Negro Tri-State Fair (Memphis, TN), 42
Negro Welfare League (Jacksonville, FL), 63, 66
New York, NY, 34, 37–38, 40
New York Harbor, 37, 40
Norman Studios, 62

Palomar Park (Los Angeles, CA), 51, 53
Paris, France, 34, 36
Pilgrim Baptist Church (Chicago), 69, 71, 72
Pittsburgh Courier, 46, 72
Powell, William J., 72, 77

Race movies, 61–62
Racism, 22, 24, 27, 28, 75. *See also* Segregation
Rogers Field (Los Angeles), 51, 76

Queen Bess. *See* Coleman, Bessie
Quimby, Harriet, 17, 19, 71

Santa Monica, CA, 52–53
Savannah, GA, 58–59
Savannah Tribune, 59
Segregation, 12, 15, 20, 24, 26, 38, 64, 67. *See also* Racism
Shuffle Along, 37–38
South Side (Chicago), 21, 22, 24, 26, 31, 39
Stroll, the, 22

Waxahachie, TX, 11–15, 18, 58
West Palm Beach, FL, 59, 63
Wills, William D., 64–66
World War I, 24–26

Acknowledgments

Illustrations are reproduced through the courtesy of: Smithsonian Institution, front cover, pp. 10, 25, 30, 33, 35, 36, 41, 44, 60, 68, 74; Schomburg Center for Research in Black Culture, back cover, p. 6; The Bettmann Archive, pp. 2, 42; Ellis County (TX) Museum, Inc., p. 12; National Archives, p. 14 (photo no. 16-G-116-1-CI-19092); Currie Ballard, Historian, Langston University, p. 16; Library of Congress, pp. 19 (LC-USZ-62-15070), 23 (LC-USZ-62-17971); Chicago Historical Society, pp. 21 (ICHi-06962), 22(ICHi-20428); *The Chicago Defender,* p. 27; Security Pacific Collection/L.A. Public Library, pp. 38, 49, 50, 70; Lilly Library, Indiana University, Bloomington, Indiana, pp. 40, 52, 57, 62; Minnesota Historical Society, p. 48; Arthur Freeman, p. 54; Florida State Archives, pp. 64, 65, 67; Hatfield Collection/Museum of Flight, Seattle, p. 72; U.S. Postal Service, p. 77.